THE RUSTLE OF LEAVES AND OTHER POEMS OF NATURE

THERE IS NO GREATER TEACHER FOR THE LIVING THAN NATURE.

DAVID T NICHOLAS

This book is dedicated to all my family members.

To all my readers who have purchased and reading this book.

This book is even dedicated to all the people in my country and around the world working effortlessly to save the environment and nature and trying to educate people on the same .

Contents

Contents

1. The Rustle of leaves

During the season of the fall
when the tree loses it all.
To the ground one by one, they just fall.
The artistic colour of the leaves
cannot be described especially of
the different shades of colour

Each leaf colour has.
The change that they go thru every day.
Thou fallen away from life astray
One should definitely spare
A minute or two during their life span
To stop, sit , stand and watch the leaves fall
During The falling of the leaves season
which Adds so much colour to the earth
when one treads upon those leaves
The Rustle of leaves is something to hear
Especially the dried crackling ones
That soon becomes composite manure.
And when the wind blows
The leaves swirl with the wind.
And if ever the wind is really harsh
The rustle of leaves one should hear then
For One may or may not get to hear them ever again.

2. There is beauty to everything

There is beauty in everything we see
There is beauty in everything we do.
For beauty is shapeless
And it takes any shape

It can be there anytime anyplace.
There are instances where
Time fades beauty or
Beauty is captured in the process of time.
Beauty is the only thing
That captivates the body, mind and soul.
The Outer Beauty that's lost from a body
This is what makes the humankind worried.
but when the inner beauty of a body is found
That beauty that is found is never lost ever again.

3. choose your own color

Every body choses their own color
In the short life span
That life has to offer to them
some choose sunny-yellow,
some choose cloudy-gray ,
some choose angry-red ,
some choose depressingly-black,
some chose mournful Purple,
whatever color we choose
we live by its own color light.
so while alive learn to
chose your own color
learn to choose it right
Because you will definitely
Live by it shadows and light .

4. The greatest teacher

The greatest teacher is nature
After all that it goes thru
From gaining everything to loosing everything
It always looks beautiful; come what may
The saddest melody one should here is
The falling of the leaves
During the season of the fall
But we don't because nature suffers silently.
The cry of nature is never heard
The sadness is never seen
Because there is beauty no matter how nature is
Its always been amazing beautiful
It looses itself everyday
As well as gains something .
There is so much to learn from nature
Many a time even nature puts us to the test
Sometime we pass ,sometimes we fail
But whatever the end result
We always learn something from nature
And learning from it will only make us live better
As nature is no doubt 'The greatest teacher'.

5. Let live the Child and Nature

Nature is a great Artist
For It knows how to achieve
The greatest effect from
The smallest of its possession
That the human mind can never imagine
But just be wowed by its beauty.
The greatness and beauty of nature comes
when it does not belong to anyone
or when its held back by someone

same as to the life of a child.
let live the child and nature
For their beauty and innocence
Will do nothing but bring prosperous love
To Mother earth and all the living
In captivity Nature is destroyed
In captivity the freedom and life of a child is lost
If nature and child are held back
Hope for the future is lost
life and its Resources are shortened
so; let live the Child and Nature
For they are meant to live but not Bound.

6. We are there too

When one sees the forest
They don't see us .
When one thinks about the forest
They don't think about us .
When one speaks about the forest
They don't speak about us .
Forgetting the fact
That we are there too .
They talk about the trees
The wild animals and the birds too.
They forget about us herbs and small plants
The micro organisms and other living things
They forget about the tiny insects and animals
some beautiful flowered plant or medicinal
some poisonous and beautiful they forget too
so who ever enters the forest
Make sure you see, think and talk about us
Just don't forget that we are there too.

7. A walk at night

A walk at night
makes you see the word differently
makes you have different
thoughts about the world .
The world at this time
becomes deserted, silent Mysterious
The thought of fear is only in your mind
once you overcome the fear of the night
there is nothing more better than
A quiet , peaceful loving walk
A walk at night .

8. Nature is Neither yours nor mine

Nature is neither yours nor mine
It belongs to all the living
For life is our nature
And nature is that which gives us
Everything that we need for life .
Nature is altruistic and so must life
Let nature Be ,what nature should be .
Not for you and you alone
But for everyone that its meant to be
Life's fullest is lived
only when lived in the midst of nature
Life's fullest is loved
Only when we love mother nature dearly
Life is fully experienced
only when one sees ,
Hears and speaks about Nature
And the most important thing is
One has to realize and truly accept
Nature is neither for one or two
Neither is nature yours or mine
It belongs to all the living

Just as a mother belongs to a child .

9. A Step towards heaven

Every step taken towards nature
Is a step taken towards heaven
For what lies in heaven no one know
Until one has seen or witnessed
So it is with nature
What lies with and within
No one knows until
He or she has experienced it for themselves
Take a step towards nature
So that you may take
Your first step towards heaven .

10. Nature's Gentleness

The wind blows gentle breeze across the land.
The water flows gently through the valley's, lakes and rivers.
The ice melts gently from the mountain top
The fire blazes gently in the fire place
The molten lava from the volcanos gently cools down
The trees are gentle in their in their place .
So must we be as nature's gentleness
For we know what happens when
Nature isn't gentle anymore ?
So never put nature to the test
In the past history tells of nature's ravages.
So always be thankful for Nature's gentleness

11. A ball of life

Earth is a big ball of life
That belongs to life itself.
The Qualities of life are Brio
It will always restore itself
And make life possible

When it's feels there is threat
To life in itself .
One life leads to another.
One life depends on another .
And life alone can bring life.
That is the universal truth of life.
Life cannot be lifeless
Or exist in a lifeless entity
So, earth is big ball of life
So be viable when upon it .

12. Circle of Life

The circle of life
It has no beginning and end .
No one know how it began
No one knows how it will end.

But it's sure we know
All things good and bad about it.
What we should ,
And What we shouldn't
What we must ,
And what we mustn't.
We must know that there
Is nothing more precious and sacred
Than the circle of life.
It must be lived and passed on
For Eternity and sacrosanct
Is that of The circle of life .

13. The beauty of a running Train at Night

Oho how beautiful is a running Train at Night.
With the random sight of burning lights
We see thru the window bright
Oho what a sight!

How musical is the sound of the running train at night.
Along with the wavy sounds of breeze.
Sometime gentle, sometime harsh.
You could even listen to a loud roar of the wind,
Oho what a sound!

And all as the train is trying to hustle.
Down towards your destination
Creating quiet a bustle.
I've experienced beauty in many ways
One of the most beautiful scene .
Is The beauty of a running Train at Night.

14. Oho Gentle Sparrow

Oho gentle Sparrow
where are you now

when i was alittle
you were so many

I would often shoo you off
till there aren't any .

so small ,short tails ,stubby powerful beaks
you brought up love like that of aphorodite

I was so young never knew so
was always happy to see a Flutter of you

Now its only sorrowful to know
that there aren't many of you

In my heart i really wished
I never shooed the host of you

Oho gentle Sparrow
where are you now

15. No greater Joy

No greater joy than seeing a seed
grow into a tiny little sappling
that you have planted
No greater joy than seeing
that tiny sappling you have grown
turn in a lovely plant
No greater than seeing the first bud

budding upon the plant
that you have planted
No greater than seeing the plant
maturing into a fine tree from
that plant you have planted
No greater joy than seeing that bud bloom
into a flower on the tree
that you have planted
No greater joy than to see that flower
turn into fruit upon the plant
that you have planted
burry a seed let it grow
and see the joy it will bring
in the seed that you have planted

16. If you were nature

If you were nature
what would you be

Would you like to be a tree
Which is earth's life key

Would you be the huge mountains
Or the mountain ranges

Would you be the ocean or the seas

Would you be rivers , lake or a small pond .

Would you be a forest or the jungle
Or a beautiful garden .

Would you like to be the bright sun
Or the beautiful stars or moon at night

for nature so many a beautiful thing
i know its would hard to choose

There are many ways
That nature can be

What we would like to be
Or what we have to be

Is To be the one to take care of nature
Just like the way it provides and takes care of us.

17. Rainbow rainbow in the sky.

Rainbow rainbow in the sky
Thy appearance I know why
I even know for When and what.
So high up in the bright blue sky
Thy seven colours of thee underlie.
Thy colours remembered best
By the Word; VIBGYOR
A view so beautiful never seen
When the skies get clean
As that of a rainbow in the sky
Especially after some heavy showers
Every age Group says with joy
Rainbow rainbow in the sky.
What aren't you always in the sky?

18. The Night

The Night is dark and slient,
Full of brightness and whispers.
If one can hear the sounds of the night
Especially the ones that sound
Aloud and alarming during the day.
One would know what essence of magic
The night has brought to us
We talk but in whispers,
We walk but tippy toe ,
We see what we imagine; fear .
We pray more and forget less.
To remember the ones we love then
That's the real beauty of the night.

19. The Air I breathe

Everyone has this in them
The air I breathe I care
The air my mom breathe I care
The air my dad breathe I care
The air my brother and sister breathe I care
The Air my loved ones breathe I care
The air others breathe I don't care
That just is really unfair
Keeping the air pure is a burden we all must bear
We must take a solemn oath and
say the air we breathe I really care
And promise to keep it pure and fair.

20. Natural phenomenon

Natural phenomena are those that
Occur or manifest without human input.
They include gravity, tides, Earthquakes,
Eruptions
Biological processes and oscillation.
Some of them are bad really bad
Some are helpful really helpful.
Most of them occur as a surprise
Comes without a warning.
Can be devastating like
That of an earthquake
The ways of nature are natural
And it's occurrence can be abrupt
So we all must learn to live
With nature and its natural phenomenon.

21. Planting a tree

Planting a tree is really good
But what's better is planting
The right tree in the right place,
Because that is what's best
For the environment and nature
We don't have to nurture the tree
Always if it's planted in the right place
Just like how other living things
Can take care of themselves
So can trees if planted at the right place
And not where human beings
Want it to be planted ; and if so
Has to be nurtured and taken good care.
Planting a tree is really good
But what's better is planting
The right tree in the right place.

22. All the trees around you

Do you know the names of all
The trees that are around you
If not ask yourselves why?
The tiny weeds and grass that grows
The plants that grow wild
And show us greenery here and there
The least we can do is take time
And know a little about them all
Because every life matters
And trees ,plants ,herbs and weeds
Have life and are living things too.
Do you know the names of all
The trees that are around you
If not ask yourselves why?

23. The Shooting star

High up in the night sky
I see the fast-moving shooting star
It's a beauty to see
Even though by distance afar
For me I call it the wishing star
For when upon seen
Was always told to make a wish or three
Whether I truly wanted to believe it or not
Was up to me but I always wished
For something dear to me
The wishes hardly got fulfilled
Just like my prayers to god
And wishes for my birthday
But still, I always believed that
A miracle or ray of hope
Is always possible when one wishes it
From the Shooting Star when seen.

24. The season of the fall

The season of the fall
is always nature's call
for some its justified
for some its not
because there is a huge loss
of completeness for the tree
it's like losing the only
cook or head chef of the family
or they are sick and bedridden
We wait till they are well
So that we can eat the good
Food cooked by them again
So is the case when the
Leaves fall from the tree
During the fall and grow back
Once again during the season of the fall.

25. The language of nature

The language that nature speaks
Has no alphabets or words
It speaks as one but speaks for all
Those that can hear will know
It mostly speaks of peace and harmony
Listen to the sound of the rain ,
Listen to the gentle wind blowing by ,
Listen to the stream passing by,
Listen to the waves that come ashore,
Listen to the whisper
Of the breeze now and then
Listen to the various sounds of the forest
Only then will you know
The language that nature speaks
Has no alphabets or words
It speaks as one but speaks for all.

26. Beauty in everything

There is beauty in everything we see
There is beauty in everything we do.
For beauty is shapeless
And it takes any shape
It can be there anytime anyplace.
There are instances where
Time fades beauty or
Beauty is captured in the process of time.
Beauty is the only thing
That captivates the body, mind and soul.
The Outer Beauty that's lost from a body
This is what makes humankind worried.
But when the inner beauty of a body is found
That beauty found is never lost ever again.
For beauty lies with whats within
And beauty can be found in everything.

27. The work of Nature

Nature is always working ceaselessly
It neither stops to take rest
Nor has a Wanderlust mind
because it understands what life
would be if it doesn't necessitate itself
we get so busy in life that we
literally forget to see the beauty of nature
The work of nature can never
Be seen or understood
Because silence and inward is it's key
Beauty and calmness are it's results
The work of Nature is not for itself
But for you and me and all living beings.

28. Winter

A season to cuddle
A season of togetherness
It is a time of comfort
It's a slow season of the year
It brings about happiness and joy
It is a time of magic, miracles, fairy tales,
warmth and new expectations
It is a great time to learn not only
To Appreciate the past, but also the future.
The cold winter has come to an end
For It always has to make way and room
For a new season that has to begin
Of all the seasons that come and go
Winter of it all will feel the longest .

29. I'm only one (pennantia baylisiana)

They commonly call me "Three Kings Kaikōmako"
I'm endemic to the Three Kings Islands,
In New Zealand, on the small Great Island
Where I'm the only plant of my species
And kind That is known to exist
I am the only one for all I know
But, I have a lot and many around me
Unlike, many of you.
With many around, but yet alone
You may feel for me that I'm alone
But feel not for me, but for thyself
For being with many but yet alone.
I have gone thru a lot in my life
Lost almost every one of my kind
But here I am standing tall
For one day I know I'll definitely fall
But, for as long as I m living
I'll provide for nature and
All that comes near me
And I teach you the same
As long you are alive

Stand tall and upright before you fall.

30. A Stream of water

A stream is a body of water
That flows on Earth's surface
A stream of water might
Be a small water carrying body
When compared to the oceans, seas and lakes
But it is as important to many
where it flows just as the
Huge water bodies.
The feeling of running your hands thru
The running water of the stream
Is just a heavenly feeling.
Streams provide many benefits to humans
They wash away waste
And provide water for drinking.
It can even help generate hydroelectricity.
It helps in fishing, boating and survival.
They most importantly provide habitat for wildlife.
A Stream of water is as important to nature
As is blood running thru our veins.

Printed by Libri Plureos GmbH in Hamburg,
Germany